Mixed Emotions

Mixed Emotions

Published by
Northern Ireland Mixed Marriage Association
28 Bedford St. Belfast BT2 7FE

Printed by
Nova Print & Design, Conway St. Belfast
ISBN 978-0-9571669-1-2
© 2012 NIMMA

Introduction

All love stories are unique and these ten accounts of mixed marriage are no exception. Each story is shared with openness and courage and, stretching back nearly seventy years, the collective experience on offer reveals much about the attitudes of the day, showing how society has changed and, yet, ironically, how it remains the same.

The challenges that society can throw at couples provide a backdrop which contrasts starkly with the straightforward acts of courtship, falling in love, making commitment and starting a family. In response, each couple demonstrates the value of tenacity and power of commitment, not only to each other, but to a better future. Their love ripples outwards across our communities and we all benefit from their triumphs.

One of the joys found within these stories is the diversity of response to common difficulties arising out of misunderstanding, turmoil and hurt. Some were subjected to outright rejection and exclusion, others to more subtle forms of coercion. Each had to make choices against backdrops ranging from violent intimidation to unacceptable familial expectations. Yet, each story sparkles with positivity. Each person tells his or her story in their own way, highlighting what is important to them. These are people who have found ways to forge a life together, sometimes with apparent ease, occasionally by serendipity and often through great courage.

They explain how they have adapted and overcome and they express the enrichment that they have experienced through mixed marriage.

Collectively, these experiences show how relationships can be made to blossom, even when it is made most difficult. People have found many different ways to embrace the positive nature of their mixed relationship and, with simplicity and honesty, they have reached out beyond the narrow negativity of others to build their own love stories.

Together, they profess how they have benefitted from mixed marriage through stories that are testimony to how much they deserve their rewards. We should be thankful that they have also shown us how, in the face of adversity, we can aspire and achieve far beyond our common divisions.

Hugh Nelson
NIMMA
February 2012.

Preface

The celebrated American journalist Mignon McLaughlin, alas no relation, wrote that 'A successful marriage requires falling in love many times, but always with the same person'. She appreciated the inevitable complications that occur in arguably the greatest and strongest of relationships, acknowledging the nuances and realities of change in people and circumstances that can cause difficulties and despair in practically any marriage. Yet, she had her own solution, love. Or rather, to keep falling in love with your husband or wife. It's not really that complicated, at least the first time. No doubt, it gets increasingly so as time goes on and if the marriage is to last, but then, when it comes to marriage of any kind, nobody said it would be easy.

It has often been said that making a mixed marriage was never easy in this country.

I came to this project knowing little about mixed marriage. I'd learnt a little about the nuts and bolts of how to make one, the logistics of the whats and hows, but had absolutely no idea of the love that is needed to ensure that one is successful. This love is not the romantic stereotype, moon/June variety, but rather the determined, persevering, self-sacrificing, compromising kind of love that brings and keeps two people together through thick and thin. The kind of love that lasts. It is out there.

I have seen it for myself, been lucky to have met the wonderful people whose stories make up this book and privileged to have been allowed to share in those stories. I hope that this resultant sharing of love and experience will be a help, perhaps even an inspiration, to all who read them.

I wish to thank all of our volunteers for their courage, their time and their warmth of welcome. I thank Meryl Spiers and Julie McLaughlin for their support and patience, all those who helped proof read the final publication, including Hugh Nelson, Ken and Maura Dunn and Anne Odling-Smee. And finally, the Big Lottery Fund and Volunteer Now whose finance made the project possible.

Paul McLaughlin
February 2012.

Mixed Emotions – Foreword

Happily unaware of any differences of culture or religion, pre-school children in mixed areas played merrily together on the streets of the cities and towns of Northern Ireland. Even when they went to primary school they noticed very few differences – perhaps some went to a school with a saint's name while others went to the local 'model' school. They continued to play together in the evenings and weekends. When they went to secondary school the differences became more obvious – whether it was the different games the schools played or the English or Irish history that they were taught, or what they had to do on Saturday mornings, whether their teachers were clergy or lay people. They began to notice differences in their school uniforms and whether they themselves joined in the parades on the 'Twelfth' or not: whether the girls appeared in First Communion dresses and the boys in little black suits or not; whether they were a family which said the rosary in the evenings or not.

If, on a rare occasion, they were ever inside 'another church' they would see different kinds of notices – in one an announcement about a Novena, or in another a warning about 'mixed marriages' being 'fraught with danger.' At a local dance a newcomer asking a pretty wallflower for a dance would be warned – 'She digs with the wrong foot you know.' Thus in the workplace or in the sports they attended - and often in the places where they shopped - they found themselves unwittingly members of a 'ghetto', so it was safer to stay in than to wander away from it and find alienation or hostility. If they formed a liaison across the 'divide' and considered the possibility of a mixed marriage, their family, their friends, their clergy would all raise difficulties and problems, and a strange rule called *Ne Temere* would be mentioned, either as a fierce direction or a severe warning.

Even when a new Papal decree *Matrimonia Mixta*, issued in 1970, eased the situation legally, the prejudices of many families, of clergy and in the wider society remained. There was very little advice, help or sympathy available, and very little knowledge of how any other mixed families were faring. It was in this situation that a few couples from 'across the divide' came together at Corrymeela to give each other mutual help and support. From this, NIMMA was born in 1974. Its original members – all volunteers – not only assisted couples who were already in, or were hoping to be in, a mixed marriage, but by a sustained campaign over decades persuaded the churches to change their official attitudes. Until relatively recently it would have been difficult and even dangerous for mixed marriage couples to draw public attention to themselves and to the fact that they had decided to put love and marriage before tribalism and tradition. While there are still pockets of resistance to be overcome and more co-operation to be achieved, this book, the first of its kind, describes how ten couples found that their love can – and did – enable them to overcome the divisions of our divided society. Even some of our politicians are now aware and prepared to state that this kind of association may well influence the way we can progress to a fully shared future.

The author, Paul McLaughlin, who has thirty years experience of interviewing in the private, public and voluntary sectors, describes himself as having 'been lucky to have met the wonderful people whose stories make up this fascinating book' and 'privileged to have been allowed to share in their stories'. The brief History of Mixed Marriage in Ireland included in this book should guide any reader to a fuller understanding of where we have been and where a shared future will take us. Individual stories of real life experiences will do much to separate fact from fiction. They speak of hope and courage, compromise and determination, and above all of how love can win through even in a segregated society.

I trust the book will be an inspiration to those who read the stories and especially to our rising generation as they learn to share with one another. We owe our contributors a great deal of gratitude for sharing their stories of how mutual love has enabled them to overcome the divisions of our divided society and may indeed point a way to a shared future.

R Edgar Turner (Canon)
Church of Ireland Chaplain to NIMMA since 1974
February 2012.

Publication of this book had long been an aim of the Northern Ireland Mixed Marriage Association (NIMMA).

It would not have been possible, however, without invaluable funding from The Big Lottery Fund and Volunteer Now and NIMMA gratefully acknowledges these contributions.

Contents

Page

Introduction	iii
Preface	v
Mixed Emotions - Foreword	vii
Say all you have to say	1
We walked the walk	8
Family is the most important thing	15
Go for it and be happy	22
We don't need to be labelled	29
You two against the rest	36
A little tolerance goes a long way	43

Contents

Page

Our love encourages respect   50

Not enough Christianity   57

Love conquers everything   64

A short history of mixed marriage in Ireland   71

Say all you have to say

Say all you have to say

Fermanagh couple Tom and Sarah, who are in their early thirties, live on a farm in the hills near Enniskillen. They both work for an electronics company in the town and their newly-built house, which overlooks Topped Mountain, has a very special occupant.

"You've got to be open-minded, completely honest and say all you have to say if you are ever going to make a relationship, maybe especially a mixed relationship, work", according to Tom, who was raised on a farm in the townland of Ballyreagh in the Fermanagh countryside.

Tom speaks quietly as 'the special occupant' of his home dozes contentedly in his chair-cum-activity centre. Seven-month-old Conor, a chatty, chirrupy bundle of fun and energy has nodded off after entertaining us.

"He's definitely the boss around this place", says Sarah, "And we're blessed to have him. He has made our house a family home."

Sarah comes from the village of Killadeas, a mainly Protestant area on the shores of Lower Lough Erne. She was raised in the Church of Ireland and has fond memories of the church and her community.

"I suppose that our social life revolved around the church and, to that extent, we would have played with mainly children of our own denomination. I don't feel this was a deliberate thing, because we had good Roman Catholic neighbours, including the lady who babysat me as a youngster, but in rural Fermanagh, like many other country areas in Northern Ireland, both sides of the community tend to spend an awful lot of their time in church-orientated activities. That's just the way things are."

Sarah went to the local primary school, but made a best friend of a Roman Catholic when sharing a bus to the secondary school.

"I'm lucky in that my Dad is English and doesn't have a lot of the pre-conceived ideas that others might and he and my mother brought us up to take people as we find them. They ran a residential home for the elderly for more than 15 years and I hope that a little bit of that caring has rubbed off on us. I know that I never felt that a person's religion would make one bit of difference to how I thought of them."

Sarah left the Lakelands for Belfast and became a business and finance student at Belfast Institute for Further and Higher Education.

"That was an education in itself. I left the beautiful and relatively peaceful surroundings of Killadeas to live in Belfast and, for two years, on the sectarian flashpoint of Roden Street between the Grosvenor and Donegall Roads. Our accommodation was cheap, and although it wasn't a very pleasant area to live in we never had any bother. I remember being shocked when my housemate told me that the neighbours probably knew everything about us, even though they'd never met us. It is a very different culture to rural Fermanagh."

Sarah had many friends of all denominations at college, and came away with a Higher National Diploma and harboured ideas of emigrating to the United States when she finished in Belfast.

" I have an Aunt and Uncle out there and I suppose the grass is always greener on the other side. Anyway, I started work in Enniskillen and fate took a hand." She looks at the slumbering Conor and suddenly the attraction of America, once so strong, is forgotten.

Tom was born and raised on a farm in the townland of Ballyreagh. It's just five miles or so from Enniskillen town, but, with no mobile phone coverage, can seem much more remote. It is a mixed area of small farms where Protestants and Roman Catholics tend to work together to the exclusion of socialising.

"The whole church thing dominates life on both sides of the divide", says Tom. "On the Catholic side, the parish is the most important thing and the social life of the area revolved around it and the Gaelic Athletic Association. Everyone gets on well, but there has always been that kind of separation."

Tom has spent all of his life in this area. Local schools, agricultural college for four years, Gaelic football for the local team. Only the 'bright lights' of Enniskillen made things look that bit different.

"My social life changed when I was old enough to travel to pubs and clubs in the town. This was much more mixed than anything I had been used to although, to tell you the truth, a person's religion was a subject that never entered my head anyway. We were having fun and religion didn't come into it."

Tom and Sarah had been workmates for nearly two years before their first date and Sarah thought a romance highly unlikely. "Of course, I'd seen him around the place, but I sat next to him at a Christmas dinner and he was a right bore with hardly two words for himself." Tom laughs at that. He did have a different girlfriend with him that evening.

Eventually, they did date – always in the relative anonymity of Enniskillen – and soon found they were in agreement. "We both knew this was something serious", says Tom, "but I felt held back by what I thought would be the reaction of my family, particularly my father, and just tried to play things by ear."

"My mother is from Dublin and reasonably open-minded, but my father has never been out of Ireland and his life has been all about this farm. It's true to say that while he has never mixed socially with Protestants, he has worked with them successfully and is a quiet country man at heart. I was sure that he would be a bit 'iffy' about Sarah and me."

Sarah and Tom even split up at one stage with Sarah taking a three week holiday in America with family and still entertaining thoughts of a new life out there. "We decided to stop seeing each other as boyfriend and girlfriend", she says, "but somehow continued to see each other just as much as before as 'friends'."

"Our break up gave us the chance, and even the little bit of space, to realise what we had together and how much we had to lose", says Tom, "and we talked a lot because we had a lot to talk about."

The results of their talking led to the decision to tell both sets of parents. "It's only natural for parents to worry about their children and mine while, of course, concerned for my happiness, wished us well. Tom was less certain that his father, in particular, would come to terms with it. "I assured Tom that once his father had got to know me, he would like me. And so it turned out. My parents think of Tom as the son they never had, while my relationship with his family could not be better."

Tom and Sarah were eventually married in the Church of Ireland church in Killadeas.

"A lot of the problems to do with attitudes toward mixed marriage and religious differences in general are to do with ignorance", says Sarah. "For instance I had never been in a Roman Catholic church and Tom had never been in a Church of Ireland church prior to our getting together and we didn't consider ourselves bigots."

"Today, I feel more comfortable with my faith and, ironically, probably more aware of it. I go to Mass sometimes and church in my home village as often as I can and I find very little differences between the two. I know what I want, I know what I believe and I realise the things that are important to me."

"We talked through as much as we could imagine before we even got engaged", says Tom. "I think it is essential for mixed couples, certainly it was for us, to be completely open and completely honest with each other, to really care about what the other person feels, to be prepared to compromise and to remember that there are no guarantees with marriage, no matter who you marry."

Sarah and Tom consider themselves lucky in that they appreciate each other's culture and denomination and took the time to learn about each other. "We were married in my church", says Sarah, "Conor was baptised in the Roman Catholic church and when the time comes for him to start school, we have already decided that the best school – no matter what denomination or none – will be our choice for him."

At that, with a gift for timing that should stand him in good stead in the years ahead, young Master Conor woke with a smile that lit up the room.

Tom & Sarah

We walked the walk

We walked the walk

Ruth is a remarkable 87-year-old widow whose husband Pat died nine years ago. She lives in a bungalow overlooking the centre of the new city of Newry and despite facing heartache as a result of her mixed marriage, found forgiveness and happiness in more than 58 years of marriage.

"I was shunned by family, friends and neighbours when I chose to marry Pat", says Ruth. "But we put our trust in God and he looked after and cared for us and our children through all our years together."

Ruth was born, the first of twelve children, on a farm near the border in 1924. "We were a happy, hard working family", she says. "My mother and father were good, decent people who set us a fine example and though the work was hard and we all had our chores, we always had plenty of food, even during the shortages of the 1930s' depression and the start of the Second World War."

"We were a Non-Subscribing Presbyterian family, my father was an Orangeman and the church, the Order and the neighbours were our community. And a close-knit community at that."

Ruth had Catholic friends as a youngster and had the rare chance, at that time, of going on to further education at the local technical college. "It was mixed" she says, "I really enjoyed it and looked forward to staying longer, but, after two years, it was decided that I would take a job as clerk in the administration section of the Armagh Down Creamery. I had no other choice."

"Again, I was part of a 'mixed' workforce and got on well with everyone, but there was little time for socialising in those days with so much to do at home."

Ruth's life was to change dramatically when she met Pat. He had been born and bred in Jerrettspass and lived in a lock house on the canal. His father laboured in the local quarry, while his mother worked the lock itself.

Ruth says, "Pat was already working at the creamery when I joined and we got talking, became friends and, eventually, started going out together. I suppose it was a normal girlfriend, boyfriend sort of thing, except that I couldn't tell anyone about him."

"We went out together for almost two years, but it was a very secretive romance, as I knew that my parents would not have approved of him. But, Newry was a small place in those days and somehow the news went round that I was intending to marry a Catholic. The first I knew about all this was the night that the local Worshipful Master of the Lodge came to our house fairly late on. I was ordered from bed, interrogated and accused. I was terrified. A young girl facing the full wrath of a man of authority. I denied everything and thought I had got away with it. The following evening, at around the same time, our Minister, who 'had it on good authority' that I intended to marry a 'Papish', cross-examined me and made me promise to break off the relationship. I still remember his words,

'May God direct you'. But he was the one doing all the directing, as well as encouraging my parents to take the same stance."

Ruth was told that she would be confined to the farm 'for good' if she did not end the engagement and she agreed to this in order to be allowed to go to work.

"I then wrote a 12 page letter to Pat, which I hoped his sister would pass on to him but, as luck would have it, I bumped into him that very day and told him everything. From that moment, I was never to return home again. We decided there and then to get married as quickly as possible."

Ruth, who had been taking instruction in a local convent for a year, had already been received into the Catholic Church.

"From then on, things moved very fast. We took a taxi to Dundalk, met with a local priest and, eventually, got the Cardinal's permission to marry on the 26th June 1943, despite the fact that I was only 19 and legally two years under the age of consent. Pat's family were very supportive, but I know that my name was never mentioned again in my mother's and father's house after I left."

"We had one day for a honeymoon and then back to Newry on the Sunday for work on Monday. I had only the clothes I stood up in and, it's funny now, but I was able to borrow a uniform from Pat's sister who was a nurse."

Ruth's and Pat's troubles were only beginning. Both found themselves without their respective jobs because of the marriage. On Pat's return to work at The Provincial Coal Company – Fisher's Coal-yard – he was told that his services were no longer required, while Ruth was strongly advised by her employer at the creamery not to recommence work as her family were pressurising them to dismiss her. Pat then had to travel to England to get work. "We wrote to each other daily", says Ruth, "as that was our only means of communication". That first Christmas, 1943, husband and wife were apart and Ruth's parents returned her greetings card and present unopened. Family disowned her and former neighbours ignored her. "As everyone had ration books at that time, I had to go to my family's grocer, Bob Mitchell, to claim my allowance. They fulfilled my order, but the transaction was conducted in silence and I was not acknowledged."

"Later, when I went to buy my first pair of new shoes in Kennedy's, our family shoe shop, they refused to serve me even though I had the cash in my hand. I felt humiliated and shocked as my family had always been regular customers."

"My father told me that I should have kept my own religion. That was it. I was no longer part of their family. They were good people, but, at that time, they wouldn't, or probably couldn't, step outside their community, with all of its constraints, to show acceptance of what I had done. I suppose that, given all the circumstances, they felt they had no other choice. I was never back in my parents' home again and did not even get my belongings."

Ruth was stopped from attending her father's wake and funeral, which she watched from a garage door in the town, and only got to see her dying mother in hospital after being smuggled into the ward. "Although my mother didn't speak to me that last evening", she says, "I did get the chance to tell her that I loved her."

Pat worked at several driving jobs, while Ruth reared their four children. Baby Ruth, their fifth child, survived for only one day. "Pat eventually went self-employed as a taxi driver, I got a job in the local credit union when the children were at school and we were able to build up our home and care for our family."

Ruth and Pat had a very active retirement, travelling to California several times and Australia, Lourdes, France, England, Wales and all over Ireland. "We used to walk a lot around Warrenpoint, Rostrevor and Omeath, talking a lot and reminiscing about our past lives, our children, our grandchildren and our great grandchildren and thanking God for all his blessings and for the good friends who stood by us during our married years."

"As I said earlier, we put our trust in God and he looked after us and our family through our married life. We had struggles and triumphs, but were happy and so much in love."

"A school friend, whose brother had married my sister, finally persuaded her to visit me when my last child was born. I was twenty years married at that time. On another occasion, Pat saw another sister downtown with her husband whom he knew and Pat suggested that we say 'hello'. Since that day, we have continued to stay in touch."

Ruth's three brothers and their wives went against the family's shunning and visited Pat when he was ill in hospital. "It was wonderful to see them and, thank God, we have maintained that contact over the years."

"I would advise any couples thinking about marrying to be true to themselves, to talk to each other and to work together. Pat's favourite sayings were, 'Ups and downs we've had a few, but here we are again', 'We walked the walk and talked the talk,' and 'We'll stick together like the ivy on the old garden wall'. We did it all together and, despite everything, I would do it again tomorrow. Times have changed for the better, but love doesn't change and that's the important thing. Oh, and by the way, the Worshipful Master who terrified me way back in 1943 – his granddaughter has married a Catholic!"

Pat & Ruth

Family is the most important thing

Family is the most important thing

Chris and Roisin, who are in their mid-thirties, live in the Oldpark area of north Belfast. Chris is a bakery worker, Roisin a supervisor in a solicitor's practice. They have been married for more than 11 years and are proud parents of seven-and-a-half-year-old Matthew. He says that the 'half' is very important.

"We keep politics out of our home", says Roisin. "In Northern Ireland it is divisive and there is no place for it in our relationship. We don't watch the news about this place and neither of us feels that any of the politicians have the welfare of ordinary people at heart." "Obviously, we have our own views on many things", agrees Chris, "we'd both lived in this society for more than 20 years before we met, so we have attitudes whether we like it or not. But, we've found that our family life is more important than religion or politics and it comes first every time."

Roisin was born in the Ardoyne area of the city and is convent-educated. She has two brothers and two sisters and lives not far from her Mum and Dad. She manages a successful solicitor's practice less than half a mile from her home and has worked there since leaving school.

"We bought this house despite the fact it was the first we had viewed", she says, "because I knew it was right and it had the advantage of being close to my parents. Family is the most important thing in my life; my husband, my son and my extended family. Oh, and it's also handy for work."

Her first memories are typical of many Belfast youngsters of her generation. "I remember bin lids being banged, deafening noise and burning. The first of the hunger strikers was dying and Ardoyne went crazy. It is not the sort of memory I would wish on any child, but in those days, where I came from, there was a constant atmosphere of tension and violence. I remember the strangeness of English accents and the constant harassment of older people in the street by the army who seemed to be everywhere, all the time."

Roisin's parents moved their family to the relative quiet of the Cliftonville Road area, but after less than five years and frequently smashed front windows, they were intimidated out of their home by loyalist paramilitaries. "It was sad and shocking at the same time, as we were forced to move back to Ardoyne after our house was bought under a vesting order, at a fraction of its cost, by the Housing Executive, but worse was to come. My father's brother was murdered in his café on the Crumlin Road by unknown loyalist killers .We were devastated and my memory of my father's tears will stay with me forever."

"I had been sheltered from the Troubles, as they're called, by my parents. They wanted only what was best for us. I'd gone from knowing no Protestants at all when I lived in Ardoyne originally to taking part in Girl's Brigade activities regularly during our five year stay on the Cliftonville Road. Then, it was back to Ardoyne again and a Catholic-only environment." Through all of this time, Roisin was involved in Gaelic games. "I have been a member of the Ardoyne GAA club for nearly as long as I can remember. I was a Camogie player for more than 20 years at all club levels and, subsequently, I have taken up coaching some of the younger girls. It is a healthy and disciplined sport and one that I love." Roisin has also enjoyed a successful county career with the Antrim team and still spends up to five evenings a week volunteering her time to help the young of her community. "The GAA was my life as a teenager: my sporting life and my social life to the exclusion of everything else I suppose. I didn't venture into town much in the evenings, so it was really by chance, on the invitation of my sister and her friend, who worked together in the Northern Ireland Civil Service, that I met Chris. But for fate, I'm sure our paths really could not have crossed."

Chris, who works in a busy North Belfast home bakery, comes originally from a townland outside the County Antrim coastal town of Larne. "We moved about quite a lot when I was a youngster", he says, "mainly around the Carrickfergus area. So, as you can imagine, I didn't meet a lot of Catholics for the first ten years of my life. I'll correct that, I didn't meet any Catholics at all." That was rectified when the family, Chris, his mum and dad and brother, Scott, moved to Newtownbreda village in the countryside to the south of Belfast as he prepared for secondary school.

"Technically our family was Methodist, but we didn't attend church and it certainly wasn't a big deal in our house, so a person's religion didn't much matter to me either way. But Newtownbreda was a mixed area and, before long, I had taken a part-time job in a local petrol station, made Catholic friends and very good ones at that."

Chris attended Newtownbreda High School and like most of the other boys gathered firewood for the bonfire and looked forward to 'The Twelfth' celebrations. "It was a season of the year, like the others we had for games and sports and one that I enjoyed, but that was it. A bit of a laugh. I wasn't brought up to be sectarian or, to be honest, even to care what anyone else 'was'. It just didn't occur to me then and it still doesn't today."

"I had been socialising in Belfast, particularly around Lavery's pub, which was totally mixed, for a few years when I first met Roisin. I already knew her sister and we all got along well."

"We got on better than well", says Roisin. "Chris and I walked and talked until five o'clock that first morning, and despite the fact that he had forgotten my Christian name by the time I rang him later that morning, I knew that this was the real thing or whatever they call it today." "I was half awake when she rang", says Chris, "I could hardly remember my own name after a night on the town."

Chris and Roisin courted for four years before marrying. Chris says, "We were party animals in those days, trouble or no trouble, and we had a great time before we eventually settled down. They were often difficult times", says Roisin. "There was tension with things like Drumcree and lots of sectarian trouble and Chris and I lived on polar opposites of Belfast. He in the far south, me in the extreme north. Both sets of parents were worried. It was only natural when you are going out at night and travelling so far, but we continued to meet in the city centre and somehow I think that adversity actually strengthened our relationship."

"Our parents were never a problem", says Chris. "They saw how we were together and were happy for us. As we have said, we are very family orientated – both sides of our family."

Chris and Roisin, whose younger sister is also in a mixed relationship, married in her local Catholic church with both families in attendance. "We had talked through what we wanted well before hand", says Roisin "and the day went well. We had also discussed our attitudes toward children long before we were married. Like most mixed marriage couples, I suppose we talked more because we had more to talk about. Chris was happy for Matthew to be baptized Catholic, because he himself has no religion, and we both recognise that our son will make his own decisions when he comes of age."

"We have always tried to compromise rather than argue", says Chris, "because we love each other and we always remember that it's easy to fall into sectarian traps. I'm not political, Roisin isn't either and, while Matthew will make his First Communion soon, religion plays little part in our home life. I just know that we got on from the start and we have kept it going. That's all the advice I could give any young people thinking about a mixed marriage."

"Yes", says Roisin, "love is love and if religion means anything, it should mean that it should never get in the way of two people in love."

Chris & Roisin

Go for it and be happy

Go for it and be happy

Katherine is a former nurse who lives in the County Armagh countryside outside the border village of Forkhill. She is a widow in her mid-70s, but with the vim and energy of a much younger woman. They are attributes that stood her in good stead in the past.

Neighbours and acquaintances had a lot to say about Katherine's budding relationship with her future husband back at the start of the 1960s. "It seems that just about everybody had an opinion about what I was doing," she says, "from the wee Catholic woman who called at my mother's house when the hairdresser's next door was shut with her comment 'Get the holy water missus for your man is as black as a pot', to the Protestant neighbours who wrote to my future mother-in-law to say that they 'had heard the dreadful news' and 'this would never have happened if her husband had been alive."

That annoyed me a lot as the last two had said to my face how pleased they were and that I was a 'lovely girl'. But I suppose that when it comes down to it, there's no limit to hypocrisy in this country. Especially back then."

Katherine and her late husband James (Junior) struggled against the intransigence of the Roman Catholic hierarchy for five years before finally being 'allowed' to wed in 1965. "We went through a heck of a lot and persevered to get married in the first place back in the 1960s", she says, "but I can tell you now that I would not be dictated to again and say to today's young people to go for it and be happy."

Katherine was born on Merseyside where her father and mother had gone in search of work, but, from the age of three, she and her four siblings, lived in the predominantly Roman Catholic village of Forkhill in South Armagh. "I went to the local Catholic primary school, then on to Sacred Heart Convent in Newry and I can remember clearly that, from my earliest days, I wanted to be a nurse. I even used to use a pillow as a patient for heaven's sake."

Katherine's dreams of a nursing career took a knock when she was struck down with rheumatic fever at the age of 15. "I was very ill for a time, but remarkably, I recovered well and, thank God, have never had any problems related to my heart." As soon as she was 18, Katherine took the boat to Liverpool to train at the city's Walton General Hospital. "It was three years of intense training", she says, "very hard work and long hours, but it was what I wanted to do and I enjoyed it." Her second spell on Merseyside, ironically the same length as her first in childhood, came to an end with Katherine qualified and going on the hunt for a job.

She says, "Those were difficult times for Catholics and, despite my seniority, I was forced to accept a temporary position at Daisyhill Hospital in Newry. That lasted three years, during which I had few rights and no paid holidays, but, eventually, I was appointed to a permanent position. It was worth the wait."

James or Junior, as he was known all of his life, died more than eleven years ago, but his memory is very much alive in the bungalow where he and Katherine spent most of their married life.

"Junior came from farming stock. They owned a place just outside the village of Forkhill and were Church of Ireland people. He worked the farm and as well as working with Catholics – it would have been practically impossible not to in this part of the country - he also socialised with them. He was well-known and well-liked and cared not a scrap about anyone's religion. He liked a drink, a dance and a bit of craic and even played football regularly across the border in Dundalk."

Katherine and Junior's paths first crossed at a dance in the neighbouring village of Jonesborough. "I'd seen him before of course, but never took any notice. Yet, that night, we just clicked and began going out together." Their courtship, however, was somewhat different from normal. "Aye, we used to meet up on the other side of the border away from prying eyes and wagging tongues. All the time, my mother knew I was seeing someone, mothers always do, but she never imagined it would be a Protestant. 'Wait until your father comes home', she said, and sure enough his contribution was short and not so sweet; 'You finish with this character or your clothes will be left at the corner'. I was 24 years old, had a very responsible job and everybody, but me, knew what was best for me."

Katherine and Junior even split up for nearly two months as a result of the pressure of the situation. "We thought it best at the time, but met up at a carnival one evening and that was that. I went home that night and told my parents, 'I'm back with James (Junior) and I'm staying with him'. Their faces were a picture, but they knew I meant it and that was the end of the opposition as far as they were concerned. I'm afraid I couldn't have said the same about my future mother-in-law. She hardly spoke to me, even when we got engaged after two years. That was when the nosey neighbours came into their own, but even the two who wrote the infamous letter I mentioned earlier were left red faced when I told them 'Our first-born will be called Paisley'. One local wag, a real old bachelor character joked about Junior turning his religion, but I told him, 'The only turning he'll do will be in bed' and we all had a good laugh."

Unfortunately, neither Katherine nor Junior had much to laugh about after that. They approached their local parish priest and requested the permission that would allow them to marry. "First of all, he assured us that there wouldn't be problem", she says, "but then told us that the new Archbishop of Armagh, Cardinal Conway, had turned us down. I met privately with the Cardinal and soon discovered for myself the cut of the man. 'You'll never get the dispensation', he said, 'so go home, find a Catholic fellow and forget about this one'. I told him that I would travel to England to marry and he said that he would stop that as well. Eventually, he relented, if you can call it that, saying that the marriage could take place in Liverpool, but I dug my heels in and kept pressing for a wedding in my home village. The best the good cardinal could say was, 'I'll remember you in my prayers'."

Ironically, if Katherine had fallen pregnant at any time during those long five years, the local hierarchy would have removed all obstacles and married them immediately. "They said that would be an 'excuse' to get married", she says, "I knew I didn't need an 'excuse'."

Eventually, with the help of a priest in Carrickmacross in Co Monaghan, the couple were granted the permission. "It should have been the happiest of times, but once again, the Cardinal attached impossible conditions. Only four people would be permitted to attend the wedding – that was us and the two witnesses – there was to be no publicity, no photographs and no music. We were devastated, but, thank God, the local priest allowed all of those and we made the best of the day, despite the fact that we were married 35 miles from home and at a side altar." Katherine and Junior had a great day with family and friends in attendance, although Katherine's mother-in-law didn't travel for health reasons. "Six months after our wedding", says Katherine, "a mixed couple from this diocese were allowed to marry in Dundalk Cathedral without any problems at all, but I think that money did more than a little of the talking in that case."

"We were blessed with four daughters who were raised Catholic, which was what both Junior and I wanted, although, disobliging to the end, the Catholic Church prevented my late husband's brother from being godfather to even one of his nieces and we were told that 'No Protestant would be allowed to stand for a child in this parish'."

Katherine and Junior were married for 35 years until he passed away eleven years ago. "Even then, we had a very ecumenical funeral. My late husband, at his request, was buried in our plot in the Catholic Mullaghbawn cemetery after a packed service in the local Catholic church at which his own Church of Ireland rector delivered the eulogy. We may have been dictated to at our wedding, but the celebration of Junior's life went exactly as we wanted."

Katherine is still a regular mass-goer despite the bigotry, as she calls it, toward her marriage by many clergy. "They were arrogant, very narrow-minded and determined to get their way and it seemed to me that things could only be different if you had money, but we were just as determined, thank God, and fought for our happiness and to a great extent, apart from the odd exception, we were accepted by all. I would say to any couple thinking about making a mixed marriage to go for it, make it all you can make it and be happy. We did and I'm proud to say that."

Katherine & James

We don't need to be labelled

We don't need to be labelled

David and Nuala are in their early forties. They have been married for nearly 20 years and have four children. David is an electronic engineer while Nuala is a classroom assistant in a local primary school. They have known each other nearly all their adult lives.

David and Nuala live in a quiet cul-de-sac on the outskirts of Carryduff, a small town to the south of Belfast. It is an area where many mixed married couples have chosen to live. "It's a good place to bring up children", says David. "A place where people get along and get on with their lives". "Yes", says Nuala, "we're lucky to have been able to make our home here, away from Belfast with all of its traditional problems, in a town where barriers have been broken down and good relationships forged."

The suburbs of County Down are a world away from the terraces of North Belfast where Nuala was born and brought up. "I grew up on the city's New Lodge Road, which was a really Catholic district in one of the worst areas of sectarian conflict in the country. I went to the local primary school and can honestly say that I would not have met or even thought about Protestants until, thanks to the hard work of my mother and father, we were able to move to a much bigger house on the Oldpark Road when I was eleven. That was a dramatic change, as there was only one other Catholic family on that part of the road, although it really made no difference to me or my four brothers and sister. We hadn't been brought up to be 'bitter' as they say in Belfast. Both my mother and late father were good decent people who had friends from both communities and encouraged us to do the same."

Nuala passed her Eleven Plus exam and for the next seven years travelled across Belfast to St Dominic's Grammar School on the city's Falls Road. "There were other good schools much closer to home", she says, "one just 10 minutes walk down the road, but those were the days when Catholics went to only Catholic schools, so I and many like me had to grin and bear it." St Dominic's was all girl and all Catholic, so it wasn't until Nuala, aged 16, got a part-time job in Woolworths that she got the chance to mix with people of other denominations. "I quickly made friends, regardless of religion, and learned what a social life was all about."

Two years later, Nuala went to Queen's University to study French and Business and found herself sharing a house with girls of all denominations and none. "Nobody cared what religion anyone was", she says, "and that's the way it should be." Nuala's first year at Queen's was also significant for the fact that at the end of it, she met David.

David was born and raised Church of Ireland on the predominantly Protestant Belvoir Park estate in South Belfast. "There were two Catholic families in the estate," says David, "but only two. That's just the way it was. I didn't think about it at all. I hadn't been brought up to have prejudices against anyone because of his or her religion, although I suppose I had heard all the usual derogatory remarks about Catholics or 'Taigs' as they were called, by the time I went to grammar school. I was lucky in that my parents were not bigoted. Both had Catholic friends. My mum's best friend, Rosemary, was a Catholic who became her bridesmaid, while my dad was a committed trade unionist who looked forward to a time when Protestant and Catholics workers could put socialist politics before bigotry."

"Very appropriate then that I should attend what was described as Belfast's working class grammar school, Annadale. It was mostly Protestant – all boys – but it did give me a good education."

David went on to Queen's University to study Electronic Engineering and, after seven years and being offered a lectureship there, gained his doctorate.

David had met Nuala on a campsite in Spain when he was a shy sixth former from Annadale and she was a 'sophisticated' undergraduate at Queen's.

"I was 19 at the time", says Nuala. "so, I suppose he was my toy boy. All I knew was that we hit it off right away hundreds of miles from Belfast and light years from the kind of sectarianism that was the norm then."

David remembers, "We travelled home on the same coach – yes, a coach from Spain to Northern Ireland – and I was disappointed that Nuala had already arranged to stop off in London." His disappointment eased when he rang Nuala's home a couple of weeks later and they started going out together.

There were problems connected with that, though geographical rather than religious. "We lived at the two extremes of Belfast", says David, "I mean North and South and without a car between us, we relied on public transport. Obviously, our parents worried about our safety in travelling across the city in such dangerous times, but we persevered and it was well worth it."

"I think we knew pretty quickly that we wanted to be together", says Nuala. "We talked about what we wanted, decided what was best for us and got on with it. Religion was never a dominant topic of conversation", says David, "we never shied away from it, but we were always positive and our families were tremendously supportive."

David and Nuala were married in 1992 at her local Catholic church, weeks after David graduated, in an inclusive service that saw David's rector, fully robed for the occasion, give the sermon. "It was a great day", says Nuala, "and one that augured well for the years ahead. Of course, we've been lucky, but we've also had to work at it – like all couples in all marriages – and the fact that our families are very similar was a bonus."

Today, Nuala and David have two boys and two girls. "We feel that integrated education is the single most important thing in helping to bring about a shared future in this country", says David. "Our children, although baptised Catholic, attend either state or integrated schools and are all the better for it. I'm not sure how they would describe themselves if they ever thought about it", says Nuala, "baptised Catholic and their activities include

Baptist Girls' Brigade, Church of Ireland youth club, Church of Ireland scouts and a Presbyterian summer scheme. As good a mix as you could wish for."

"Being in a mixed marriage has certainly influenced how we feel about organised religion", says David. "We don't have a need to have either ourselves or our children labelled as one thing or the other. We are bits of all and we want our kids to dip into everything and just be happy."

"The rituals and discipline of organised religion dominated a lot of my early life, but, even with the best of intentions, this was not what we wanted for our boys and girls."

"I would advise any young couple thinking about making a mixed marriage to have the courage of their convictions, to stay true to themselves and to follow their instincts", says David, "and to cultivate their good, black, Northern sense of humour."

"Most of our friends, half of whom are in mixed marriages, enjoy the craic and banter of slagging each other off about religion, about 'Prods and Taigs' and all the rest of it. That's the way it should and can be in a 'normal' society. It's fun and its healthy and, better still, it's harmless. We look forward to the day when it's like that right across the country."

David & Nuala

You two against the rest

You two against the rest

Martin and Sharon, who are both in their forties, are from Derry/Londonderry, have been married for nearly 30 years and have two grown up children. Martin is a successful businessman and runs a tour company in the city. They are a hardworking team and a resilient couple that has faced down both poverty and the violence of sectarian opposition.

Martin and Sharon live in a quiet suburb of the maiden city. Their home exudes peace and contentment, but it is a world away from the turmoil of the early years of their relationship. "We really went through the mill," says Martin, who has spoken on mixed marriage on both BBC and Channel 4 television, "but we have a better and stronger marriage as a result. It is amazing, but this is the first time that we have sat down as a couple and actually talked through our time together, never mind to anyone else, but it has been very positive and we want to pass that on to other couples who are considering mixed marriage. Thugs, bigots and all those who simply turned away couldn't break us and, arguably, made us all the more determined to make a go of it. It was always us against the world."

Sharon is a quiet, thoughtful woman who remembers the past slowly, almost reluctantly. "I was born and raised on the Fountain Estate. Before the "Troubles", around 13,000 Protestants lived on this side of the River Foyle, today there are less than a thousand. I suppose you can see where the siege mentality comes from now, but back then it was a bigoted place where Roman Catholics, far from being welcomed, would have been in physical danger."

Today, the only peace wall in the city separates the Protestants and Roman Catholics that live on this bank of the river. "When I was growing up, there were no Catholics living on our estate, although some did attend my school, Templemore Secondary. In fact, my best friend there was a Catholic. There would have been a definitely anti-Catholic attitude in our district, with all the bands, flags and bigotry that goes with it but, thankfully, I didn't have a problem with anyone's religion or lack of it. I didn't then and I don't now."

Sharon left school at 15 and started work at the local 'Rollerdrome'. "Martin and I worked there together and, although I probably knew that I was the only Protestant in the place, I didn't think about his religion when he asked me out."

Martin is a confident, articulate man who has spoken at length about mixed marriage, but considers this opportunity too good to miss. "It's all well and good recording 60 or 90 minute pieces for television", he says, "but the final edited versions are at the whim of a director and most of what is important is lost as he looks for a sensational sound-bite. At least, that's how I've found it and I haven't heard others speaking up for themselves or people like us."

Martin comes from the Catholic Creggan Estate in the city and, as a boy, admits that he did not even meet Protestants. "It just didn't happen. We lived in different worlds. There were no Protestant friends because there were no Protestants. My father, who was a bookmaker, would have had acquaintances and work associates of different religions in the business part of his life, but we boys had no contact, never socialised, never mentioned and never thought about people from the 'other side'. I even had to make a long detour going to school to avoid a Protestant area, ironically a stone's throw from where I live today, to avoid being beaten up on a daily basis. One of our teachers, who lived locally, kept a watch out for us and made sure that we were safe. It was a violent and bigoted time, but one that we were all used to."

Sharon was 15, Martin 17 when they started going out together. "From the start, it was a difficult situation and the threat of violence was always there with a crowd waiting for me on more than one occasion", says Martin, "so, our courtship was probably shorter and more intense because of that. We just put two fingers up to everybody and got on with it. Everything we did, we did quickly because we felt rejected and pressurised."

Martin rented a sparsely furnished flat to get away from home and within a short time Sharon, under pressure at home and from her neighbours, moved in. She remembers, "I didn't associate with the people on the estate, but I was still regarded as a 'Fenian lover' and was the butt of abuse and hassle. It was good to get away from that." Martin says, "It was us two against the world."

The couple married in the registrar's office of the city's Guildhall with some family in attendance. "My mum and dad went and one brother and one sister", says Sharon, "and we went back to my parent's house for tea and sandwiches afterwards. "Yes, it was poor", says Martin. "We hadn't issued any formal invites and Sharon wasn't worried about missing out on a 'big day' and I suppose we were regarded as two renegades in this part of the world."

Times were hard for the young couple – Martin was 19, Sharon 17 – and started from day one. "We spent two nights, our honeymoon, in an ancient caravan at rain-lashed Benone strand", says Sharon, "soaked to the skin and with the use of an outside toilet."

Housing was their first priority and, despite getting a home four miles outside the city on a mixed estate, Martin was to find that his real troubles were only beginning, "We loved the house and the area and the local people were okay, but access to the estate meant passing through a loyalist district and that was to prove painful." Martin was attacked on a number of occasions during the next five years as he moved from job to job to build a life for them, but eventually, after a police recommendation, the couple were housed in the mixed Northland area of the city. They still live in the same house today.

"It was a Godsend", says Sharon. "We felt safe and now faced all the problems that every couple faced in those days, but without the sectarian one to make things worse."

Martin says, "I was always a risk taker. I opened a wee shop, worked all the hours God sends and still found that it failed. Sharon was for giving up and playing it safe, but I went in again head first, with the backing of a Coleraine wholesaler, and eventually made it work. But, 12 to 15 hour days over sixteen years take their toll and we both decided to sell up a few years ago. We had done well and, in the meantime, spotted a niche in the market to cater for the growing number of tourists who came to the city. We started the Derry City Tour Company and it has gone from strength to strength."

"I try to guide visitors on an 'unbiased' tour of the city", he says, "and I'm sure that my background in a mixed marriage is a big help to me. I feel that I have got both perspectives when it comes to the history of this place." Martin and Sharon have two grown up daughters. She says, "the girls were baptised Catholics. I don't practice my religion, but I still regard myself as a Methodist. They went to integrated primary and secondary schools and are a credit to us today."

Martin agrees. "Like us, our girls have a wide circle of friends of all religions and none and we are all better people for that. This mixed marriage thing has been an enlightening experience for Sharon and me. I suppose it's given us a broader outlook than we would have had had we stayed in the ghettos. It has certainly made us more understanding of the other person's point of view."

"If it has taught us anything", says Sharon, "it has shown us that we are all the same and that religion, the great divider as far as I'm concerned, shouldn't come into it."

"Yes", says Martin, "we went through terrible times where our private lives seemed to be the business of every bigot in this city, but we are stronger for it and I would strongly advise any couple contemplating mixed marriage to go for it regardless of what other people think. At the end of the day, it is you two against the rest if needs be. And those two are the most important people in any marriage."

Martin & Sharon

A little tolerance goes a long way

A little tolerance goes a long way

Roley and Jo live on the outskirts of the quiet village of Ederney in the beautiful Fermanagh countryside. "Close enough to walk to the shops and far enough away from the neighbours not to hear me guldering at the kids", according to Jo. Roley is a civil servant, Jo works in a local school. They have been married for more than 25 years and have four children.

"Getting into a mixed marriage has proved an education for both of us", says Roley. "Previously, we knew nothing of each other's church and very little of each other's culture. We have learned a lot and, perhaps more importantly, found that love, when it has to, can really break down barriers and overcome all opposition." "We learned to share and to be tolerant", says Jo, "and that a little bit of Christianity goes a long way."

Jo, don't call her Josephine, was born and bred in the predominantly Roman Catholic village of Ederney. She was the baby of the family. "I didn't have Protestant friends when I was growing up", she says. "It wasn't a conscious decision, there just weren't any around. As a result, I suppose that I had no reason to think about religious differences. They didn't exist for me as a child in that environment."

That changed when, after school, Jo took a job at Desmond's clothing factory in the nearby town of Irvinestown. "It was all new to me, like it is for any teenager starting work, but, for the first time, I found myself in a place that was truly mixed. And I loved it. I made friends from both 'sides', we went to mixed dances and had boyfriends of both religions just like normal people. Changed times! My best friend throughout the best part of my life has been Allison, a Protestant."

Jo continued to live in the village and cared for her father in the family home.

Roley was born a couple miles from where he now lives, in the Lower Lough Erne village of Kesh, which was mainly Protestant. "I was Church of Ireland", he says, "and lived with my mother and grandmother. My grannie was like a mother to me as my own mother had to go out to work to support us. It was a happy childhood in a home that had an open door for everyone, regardless of religion. In fact, religion was something that was practised on a Sunday and never mentioned again during the week. I had friends of both persuasions, went to 'tech' with them as well and had a first hand knowledge of mixed marriage through my aunt who was married to a Catholic. I never saw a problem or heard a word of trouble."

Roley joined the Northern Ireland Civil Service in 1972 and swapped the rural idyll of Fermanagh for a Belfast steeped in sectarian conflict. "I shared digs on the Lower Newtownards Road in the city near a notorious interface and got my first taste of bigotry. It stank."

Roley spent three years on that CS posting, a stint that included the infamous Workers' Strike of 1974. "Those were hairy days where we were living in a tight working-class Protestant area and we had to walk up and down the disused County Down railway line, to and from Stormont, to avoid road blocks that would have prevented us from going to work. For me, it was a culture shock. I just wasn't used to living on that sort of frontline."

Roley returned to Enniskillen in 1975 to find that the impact of the 'Troubles' had spread. "There was increased division back home", he says, "I think mainly down to the IRA campaign of targeting members of the UDR, which lead to suspicion and mistrust."

Roley also worked in the Department of Social Security on Belfast's Falls Road for a period during the 1980s. "It was a difficult time", he says. "The ordinary people were the best in the world, just as I had found in East Belfast, but paramilitaries ruled the roost and violence was commonplace." A man was shot dead in Roley's workplace and because he was a trained counsellor, he was able to lend support to traumatised staff. "It was truly terrible in the real sense of the word and I will not forget the fear, disgust and horror that I and my colleagues, many of them young girls, were forced to experience."

Roley's return to work in Fermanagh brought bad news from his local GP. By now his weight had crept up to 42 stone and the doctor's advice to the then 29 year old was 'don't look forward to your 31st birthday – you won't be here'. That stark warning and the support of his family, particularly his grandmother, led to a dramatic change in lifestyle that saw him lose 29 stone, but he is quick to credit Jo's contribution to his survival.

"I met Jo about a fortnight after my grandmother passed away", he says, "and already I was heading back into the old ways of eating and drinking. I was on a slippery slope until Jo and I got together and I found that I now had a very special person in my life."

"I can honestly say that religion didn't come into it when Roley and I started going out together" says Jo. "We liked each other and took it for granted I suppose. Roley's family were fine. I was in his mother's house many times before we got engaged and was welcomed warmly and genuinely, while my father, after he had been reassured that I was not going to leave him on his own, became like a father to Roley. We were lucky in that respect." Roley interrupts, "It was a privilege to help look after Johnny, Jo's dad, who lived with us after we got married. He was a decent man and the only father I had ever known."

Others, outside the family, didn't approve of the couple's decision to marry. "Some friends, boys that I'd known for years, boys that I would have shed blood for, made it clear what they thought of a 'fenian lover'. I got Mass cards and sympathy cards through the post and a lot of silence as I was shunned by former mates. It was sad certainly, but I'll take love over ignorance any day and, anyway, most of the same boys have mellowed with time." Surprisingly, even one local Church of Ireland clergyman was less than helpful when Roley went for his Baptism lines. "Ach, he was obstreperous and ignorant and all because I was getting married. Stupid man."

The couple were married in the local Roman Catholic church, St Joseph's. "A beautiful place", says Roley, "and my own minister stole the show at the reception with the best wedding speech I've ever heard. I'm glad I have it on video."

Jo and Roley went to both churches in the first ten years after they married. They had four children, fostered nearly two dozen more and it was Roley's wish to be totally involved in the lives of his children, including their communion, that led him to convert to Catholicism about 15 years ago.

"I always said I would like to take communion with my youngsters and I am very proud of the fact that I converted. I retained my great faith in Jesus Christ, I still read the bible everyday and I have thrown myself into my local church." Roley has also become the first lay person to chair the Board of Governors at his local Roman Catholic primary school, while he and Jo still attend the Church of Ireland for festivals like the Harvest Festival.

"We celebrated 25 years of marriage this year", says Roley, "so we must be doing something right. We have a great family and have done our best to teach our children, who have benefitted from secondary integrated education, to take people as they find them and to respect other people's points of view. In the end, it is all about respect."

"Yes", says Jo, "all obstacles can be overcome by love, commitment and actually caring about the other person as much as, if not more than yourself. A little tolerance goes a long way."

"We have been very lucky in our lives", says Roley, "and we do our best to try to put something back. I hope that this book will make people see, particularly young people, that love doesn't have a denomination."

Roley & Jo

Our love encourages respect

Our love encourages respect

Stephen and Sharon live in a small village in the Fermanagh lakelands. They have been married for five years. Stephen, whose father was killed in the 'Poppy Day' bombing of Enniskillen, has suffered severe ill-health as a direct result of being in the same explosion. Sharon, whose Mum died only days before this interview, works in retail in the town. They make a strong team that faces the future with hope and humour.

"Mixed marriage is all about compromise", says Sharon, "we have learned to compromise and, hopefully, one day we will be blessed with children and will be faced with more decisions and more compromises about their upbringing." "Yes," says Stephen, "trying to see the other person's point of view helps us all to see that little bit better."

Sharon was born in Bantry in County Cork, but spent nearly all of her primary school years in Surrey where she had friends of different religions and races. "Those things weren't considered important in England, but we came to live in Enniskillen when I was about 10 and I learned that they do things differently over here. It was a culture shock."

Sharon lived in an all-Catholic street, attended an all-Catholic primary school and had no Protestant friends. "It took me a while to get used to this. I had always been brought up to take people as I found them and to treat everyone the same, but when I went on a holiday to England and brought back little presents of pencils for my schoolmates, the pencils with the rubbers on the top, I found that I couldn't hand them out. They had Union Jacks printed on them and the local schoolteacher, a well-known Nationalist, would have had a fit. It's sad. Something so simple, taken so seriously. Petty really."

Sharon was lucky in that she was chosen as a 16 year old student at Enniskillen's Mount Lourdes convent to take a cross-community trip to America as part of the Ulster Project to the United States. "It was a life-changing experience", she says. "Six Protestants and six Catholics spending four weeks thousands of miles from 'The Troubles'. Our American host families were great and we all bonded. These people, who had been strangers to me, became like extended family within a very short time. I'm glad to say that we still keep in touch with all of them."

Sharon gave up the chance to go to university when her late mother suffered a heart attack, but has no regrets. "I chose to stay to help look after Mum and I'm glad. I went from my old part-time Saturday job in retailer 'Next' to full-time in the same branch. I had all the comforts of home, as well as plenty of money and my own car. And I got to appreciate my parents. What more could you ask?"

Stephen was born in Enniskillen into a forces' family. "My late father was a station sergeant in the Royal Ulster Constabulary, while my mother served in the Ulster Defence Regiment. Several other members of my family, who were also in the security forces, were killed during

'The Troubles'." As a boy Stephen had friends of both denominations. "We moved about a fair bit in the early days and lived in predominantly Protestant areas", he says, "but, I didn't choose my friends by their religion. I wasn't brought up like that. In fact, my best friends, the Byrne boys, were Catholics."

Stephen's father retired from the force in 1985 and father and son grew closer. "I'm sure that my childhood had been overshadowed by the fear that something bad would happen to my father, my mother or my brother. They were all on the front line against terrorism at one time or another. That eased when dad left the RUC and life looked brighter than ever."

All that ended tragically, when former sergeant Samuel Gault was among eleven people killed in the Provisional IRA's bombing of the Remembrance Sunday gathering in Enniskillen in 1987. Stephen, who had just turned 18, was standing beside his father when the explosion occurred.

"Initially, when I came round, I could hardly see because of the dust and I still remember the choking sensation. My father was lying at my feet and I knew straight away that he was dead. For about a week or so I was in a daze, but my mother was fantastic. One minute, she had had a husband, next she had nobody. She was on her own, but she handled herself with dignity and helped us through those tragic and traumatic circumstances. I remember the wake and the Catholic people who came to offer their condolences. One man said to me, 'These people didn't do this in our name'. I knew he was right and listened when my mother said, 'You can't get drawn into any sort of trouble or with any bad people in retaliation for what happened. You have to live your life'."

Two weeks after the bombing Stephen developed psoriasis which has since developed into psoriatic arthritis. "During the past 24 years", he says, "I have undergone every treatment available for both conditions. Sharon injects me twice a week with the latest of these drugs. It is not a cure, but it does give my joints a bit more freedom of movement."

Before Stephen started this treatment in 2006, he was unable to walk or drive and virtually bed-ridden. "Sharon had to dress and feed me and it was a dark time. I still suffer depression, sleep deprivation and anxiety after all this time and I know that what I am going through is a direct result of the bomb on 8th November 1987."

Sharon and Stephen met in Enniskillen Golf Club in 2003. "We got chatting", she says, "Stephen knew my Dad without knowing me and we realised that we had actually lived very close to one another when we were younger. We started going out together and that was it." "Yes", says Stephen, "there was no talk of religion. We liked each other and religion didn't come into it."

"Religion was never an issue for us", says Sharon, "but it was for other relations in our families. The funny thing is that it was the actual wedding ceremony, rather than the marriage itself, that caused the most 'concern'. Church or chapel, priest or minister? That kind of thing. To be honest, we believe that it was more to do with 'what will the neighbours say' and not the fact that we were about to become a mixed marriage couple."

"Our mixed marriage is probably different from many others because Stephen's family was directly affected by the violence and I am sure some people had a lot of reservations about Stephen marrying a Catholic girl from Cork."

"We learned to deal with the disapproval of others", says Stephen, "not friends or family, but from outsiders and strangers. And I'm glad we did. If you are lucky enough to find your soul mate, regardless of religion, colour or race, you shouldn't think twice about marriage. Just go for it."

Sharon and Stephen married in Rossorry Church of Ireland with both families attending and both clergy playing their parts. "An aunt from England had suggested we marry in Spain", says Sharon, "I suppose she thought she was giving good advice, but, thank goodness, we ignored it. We had a great day to be proud of."

Stephen says, "Advice is all well and good when it comes from the right source. I would urge couples to contact the Northern Ireland Mixed Marriage Association (NIMMA), as well as their own clergy. Families think that they are doing the best for you by offering advice and support on what they think is right. However, it may be right for them, but not right for you. Go to the people who know about these things."

"We were lucky with our family backgrounds and the way we were brought up", says Sharon. "We were aware of each other's religion and respect each other's beliefs. Our love encourages that respect and we now attend and participate in each other's church services regularly." "I think it's not about what church you go to", says Stephen, "but who you go with and the love you bring with you that really counts."

Sharon & Stephen

Not enough Christianity

Not enough Christianity

Michael and Shirley live in a quiet cul-de-sac in Glengormley on the northern outskirts of Belfast. It is a mixed area. They are an outgoing, friendly and fun-loving couple who work as psychiatric nurses in the community. Both are in their late forties.

"No matter what, if you really love each other, that love will conquer all", says Shirley when asked what advice she would give to couples contemplating making a mixed marriage. Michael echoes those sentiments, but says that hard talking has a major part to play in making any relationship, particularly a mixed one. "Talk to each other, talk to your peers, talk to everybody openly and honestly", says Michael, "and that openness will pay dividends." They have been married for more than seven years and their story is testimony to that openness.

Shirley was born in the tiny County Antrim seaport of Portballintrae and raised in Bushmills where she attended the local primary and grammar schools.

"I come from a family of three girls and Mum and Dad and my sisters would have been regular churchgoers at St John the Baptist Church of Ireland in the predominantly Protestant village where I was also a Sunday School teacher for a while."

"My father would have regarded himself as a very loyal Protestant. He was a member of the Loyal Orders, the

Orange and the Black, as well as the Freemasons but, as he worked in the retail trade, he had many dealings with Roman Catholics and would have been tolerant enough of them in his own way. I remember him occasionally saying things like 'He's all right for a Catholic' about someone or other. That was the way it was then. A grudging respect I suppose. Mum's aunt had married a Roman Catholic many years before and gone to live in London and she visited my mother and father over the years. This was a normal family thing, but maybe that marriage situation was only really possible then outside Northern Ireland."

"I was never brought up to hate anyone for his or her religion and, like many another teenager, spent a lot of time at Kelly's in Portrush where we danced away our weekends without ever wondering what religion anyone else was."

Shirley left home at eighteen to travel to Belfast to train as a student nurse and soon found herself part of the intense camaraderie that was Purdysburn Hospital in the 1980s.

"I'd decided that this was what I wanted to do and really enjoyed my time there. I even met a young man called Michael, who was also a student nurse, and we began what would develop into a long-lasting friendship that took several twists and turns along the way. I didn't attend church in Belfast. There was so much else to do, but I did when I returned on visits home."

"I did actually get engaged to a Roman Catholic and brought him to meet my folks. They 'accepted' him to an extent, but somehow thinking back, I don't believe my father ever thought for one minute that I would marry him. In the end, we grew apart. That had nothing to with any religious differences."

Michael jokes that he was born on the 'wrong' side of the Newtownards Road in Belfast. His father ran a grocer's shop across the road from St Matthew's Roman Catholic church on the edge of a strongly Protestant area.

"A few Catholics lived on our side, but trade was very scarce during the marching month of July", he says, "and redevelopment came at a good time in the early 1960s when we moved to another shop in the Clonard district of the city. We were happy there, my two brothers and I served on the altar in the local monastery while my father, who could be described as a true social democrat, was well respected. We lived above the shop and manys the time he would have opened up in the small hours of the morning to make sure that no customer was left without staples like bread and milk."

"My father's father and grandfather had served in the Royal Irish Constabulary before partition and in the late 1960s he had two cousins who were serving members of the Royal Ulster Constabulary. One of them was a station sergeant just half a mile away on the Springfield Road. The onset of the Troubles caused upheaval for our family and the burning of Bombay Street around the corner from us was just the start. We were forced to move, not by loyalist mobs I have to say, after my father refused to ban police and soldiers from his shop. Our house was paint-bombed, then my father's car daubed and we moved to the relative safety of Norfolk Parade off Belfast's Glen Road. Ironically, before the Troubles, that was where the majority of Catholic policemen lived."

"I grew up attending the local Christian Brothers' Grammar School and I have no horror stories on that score. I got a good education and have fond memories of trips to the Gaeltacht in Gweedore. I turned down the chance to go into catering at the college in Portrush, took exams at Belfast's College of Business Studies and eventually the road led to Purdysburn, student nursing and the beginning of lifetime friendship with Shirley."

Michael married his first wife Theresa at 22. "Theresa's mum had been a convert and was as Catholic as can be with shrines and statues and holy pictures all over the place, but Theresa had aunts, uncles and cousins who would have been terrified of that stuff. Northern Ireland is such a strange place that I suppose that, not too far under the skin, we are all mixed to a certain extent."

Sadly, Theresa died at just 37 years of age and Michael was left alone. Well, not quite alone as he says, "I always had good friends and I remember at some of the darkest times before Theresa was so ill, Shirley and her sister would take me out for the evening and, better still, make sure I got home okay. They were true friends."

Shirley remembers. "I was at Michael and Theresa's wedding all those years before and also at her funeral. Michael came to my father's funeral just six weeks after

Theresa passed away and I appreciated his support despite his own pain of bereavement. We were there for each other."

Michael and Shirley's relationship developed over time, but even workmates who shared office space with them were unaware that they were 'walking out together' as Michael puts it. "I'm afraid their observation skills were poor as one of our bosses commented."

Michael and Shirley went on to get engaged, courtesy of a 'champagne and roses' proposal on both knees after Michael had first asked Shirley's mother for her daughter's hand in marriage. His father had called it 'observing the proprieties'.

"We were open with everyone once we had decided that we wanted to spend the rest of our lives together. That meant my family, Michael's family and, importantly, Theresa's family."

So it was that six months later, all three families were present when Church of Ireland rector the Rev Oliver Thompson, assisted by Roman Catholic priest Fr Dan Whyte, celebrated their marriage in Shirley's home church. Fr Dan was invited to share in the marriage by Mr Thompson.

"We are older and hopefully a little wiser than many young people who contemplate mixed marriage and our openness with each other and other people, which can probably be attributed to both our upbringing and our professional training stood us in good stead", says

Michael. "I'm fairly sure that my mum and dad would have preferred me to have married in a Catholic church, but we knew what we wanted and it went really well. My little niece, Theresa's brother's child, was our flower girl and all the children who have grown up with us have been very supportive."

Neither Michael nor Shirley is complacent about how things have turned out.

"We have been lucky because of circumstances. Our age, our friendship, even our families and a shared sense of humour that a psychiatric nurse must have to survive, have all helped us get through. We want other couples, maybe younger, maybe not, to see that, at the end of the day, a mixed marriage like any marriage is all about love and that", as Michael says, "sometimes, there's too much religion and not enough Christianity."

Shirley & Michael

Love conquers everything

Love conquers everything

Ann and Stephen live in a beautiful lake-front house in County Fermanagh. Stephen, originally from Belfast, is a former engineer and entrepreneur, while Ann, who was born and raised in Enniskillen, retired recently from a teaching career. They have been married since 1975, have two sons and a growing family of grandchildren.

"Mixed marriage can nearly be defined as an appreciation of each other's cultures", says Stephen. "We are culturally different in many ways, but similar in others and it is about achieving balance through listening, talking and compromise. I can't stress too strongly the importance of education in helping to develop an understanding of difference." Not surprisingly, Ann agrees. "We have based our marriage on mutual understanding and always encouraged our children to tolerate all creeds and none and to accept people for who they are and not what religion they are. We have made a successful mixed marriage and we want to show that love conquers everything."

Ann, one of five children, was born and raised on a mixed council estate in Enniskillen. Her mother was a devout Catholic, but her father, a former British soldier, was not a regular churchgoer. "I grew up in a mixed area and had friends from both sides – although we didn't think about 'sides' at all. My mother was the religious one and made sure we went to Mass and the sacraments, while my father, who was sport mad, looked after our leisure activities. I can tell you which was more fun. I went to convent school and, from an early age, teaching was always going to be the option. I loved sport and the thought of combining the two made bearable even having to leave home to train as a teacher in Belfast."

Ann is modest about her sporting prowess. She is a former canoeist and represented Ireland at the Munich Olympics in 1972 while studying for her degree in English and PE at the University of Ulster at Jordanstown on the outskirts of Belfast.

Stephen, one of four children, came from the Donegall Pass area of Belfast. It was and is a predominantly Protestant area. "It was a respectable, working class district", he says, "and my family were of good Protestant stock. My father was a plater in the shipyard and an elder in Townsend Street Presbyterian Church where we worshipped every Sunday. Sunday was an austere kind of day in our house as it was in many others across the city in the 1950s and 1960s. A day for religious observance. Dad was a hardworking and fair man and I'm proud to say the best man I've ever known."

After the local primary school and two years at Rosetta primary school in the middle-class Mount Merrion area of the city, Stephen went to Methodist College.

"I always had a sideline going to make a few bob while I was growing up. I sold sticks round the doors for a long time and even had three boys working for me before I was eleven years of age. It was a great time until I went to the grammar school. Suddenly, I found myself a working class boy at 'Methody' who preferred Soccer to Rugby. It just wasn't the right place for me."

"My friends were the local lads I had grown up with in our street and, although there were some Catholics living in the area then, none of my friends was Catholic, just as none of my friends was middle-class."

Stephen enjoyed a very successful 'second' business venture during these years as the assistant of a local man who provided flowers and foliage for retailers as far away as England. "I was making great money", he says, "and loving every minute of it. Travelling the country and learning about business long before I ever went to Belfast's College of Business Studies."

Ann met Stephen at Jordanstown while they were both in further education. "It was funny at first", she says, "because, as a result of a misunderstanding of our surnames, I thought Stephen was a Catholic and he assumed that I was a Protestant. We were both wrong and we didn't care. We got on great and started courting seriously."

"Yes", says Stephen, "we knew fairly quickly how we felt about each other. Finding out how other people felt came a little more slowly as, initially, we didn't tell our families anything."

"My mother knew that I was courting, as all mothers do", says Ann. "Her reaction to it being with a Protestant was that of a worried parent. 'It won't be easy', she said, 'we'll support you, but maybe it would better all round if you married one of your own'. My answer with all due respect was, 'You don't pick them off the shelf'. That was the end of that and, from then on, I had the full support of my family."

Stephen's father had already given him the 'inquisition' about his girlfriend, including the classic line, 'What foot does she kick with?' "My parents were trying to protect me and even my mother asked 'Who's going to turn?' I explained that neither of us was going to turn, but that we were going to get married. I was going to marry 'My famous Fenian from Fermanagh' – so called because of her Olympic achievement."

Getting married was to prove more complicated than either of the couple anticipated.

"The local senior Catholic cleric made it clear that he would not 'allow' us to be married in the main church of St Michael's in Enniskillen", says Ann. "That was our family church and the natural choice for a bride from our area, but he was adamant. He said, 'Those of my flock who are heading in the wrong direction will not be given the opportunity to parade their bad example'."

"Adamant? The man was as near to the Anti-Christ as I'll ever want to meet", says Stephen. "He was rude, bigoted and small minded and actually said, 'We don't allow mixed marriages here'. He had the power and we had no choice but to marry in the much smaller St Mary's Church in the small village of Lisbellaw."

"We talked about the differences in culture at the start and that was evident at the reception where the Catholics seemed much more at home with the celebrations", says Stephen. "Both our families were there to support us, but my mother was very reluctant to dance with me, even though it is traditional. I thought perhaps it was the 'mixed marriage' thing bothering her. She did get up eventually, but stood like a ramrod throughout and was relieved when the music finished. On asking her, I was glad and sad to discover that it had nothing to do with Ann and me. This was the first time my mother had ever been on a dance floor."

Ann, who taught in a Catholic school at the time of her marriage, says, "The local clergy weren't happy about it – one of 'their' teachers marrying a Protestant, but, thankfully, I had already arranged to move jobs to a state school."

"Making a mixed marriage is probably the hardest thing I have ever done", says Stephen, "but it is definitely the best thing. In life, you have to be true to yourself and honest with others and if that means leaving your comfort zone, then so be it. I would advise any couple to follow that rule, not to hesitate and to go for it."

Ann and Stephen are not part of any organised religious group. "We were put off by the bigoted attitudes and negative experiences of people on both sides of the divide", says Ann, "and Stephen, in particular, found the Catholic Church unwelcoming, negative and entrenched, but we compromised all the time to get what was right for us and our family. We had our boys baptised Catholic, but not confirmed, and sent them to state schools and they have turned out a credit to us. I like to think we have handed on a flame of tolerance as bright as any Olympic one."

Stephen, Ann and their seven grandchildren

A SHORT HISTORY OF
MIXED MARRIAGE IN IRELAND

A SHORT HISTORY OF MIXED MARRIAGE IN IRELAND
By Ken Dunn, Chairman of NIMMA

For the last century marriage in Ireland between Protestants and Roman Catholics has been a very contentious issue, not fully understood by many. To understand and appreciate the depth of feeling about mixed marriage it is helpful to look at the historical background. Since space is limited, the review will be brief with salient features highlighted. Some additional reading material is appended for those who want further details.

Ken Dunn, Chairman of NIMMA

The early Church followed the marriage custom of the Roman Empire. The ring, the bride's veil and the exchange of promises that we know today all come from pagan Roman betrothal and marriage customs. The young couple announced their betrothal and on the appointed day there was a procession from the bride's parental home to the new matrimonial home for food and dance. The custom then developed that the procession would detour past the Church where the priest would come out, give a blessing and join the procession.

Such a system is very open to abuse – his word against hers. A man could walk out and journey a dozen villages away and start again! Thus, from the 11th century, the Church began to require that the couple exchanged their marriage vows before three witnesses; a priest and two lay people. A system still in use today. This practice was formalised at the Council of Trent (1563) in a document called *Tametsi* (nevertheless). This was enforced only where it was promulgated. Ireland was very patchy.

Ulster	late 16th century
Tuam	1658 - 1745
Cashel	1785
Rest of Ireland	1827

Thus in the 264 years from 1563 to 1827 Ireland had time to develop its own approach to mixed marriage.

With the coming of the Reformation, we have 'mixed marriage', i.e. marriage between a Roman Catholic and a Protestant. Originally mixed marriage laws referred to marriage with a pagan and required that the children be Catholic. At the Reformation, the Protestants were considered pagans and the same should apply. In Europe, most countries followed the denomination of the ruling King or Prince.

In the Spanish Netherlands in the 1590s, *Tametsi* was used to persecute the Protestant population:

"The most effective weapon in eliminating the Protestants was the proclamation that marriages celebrated by Protestant pastors were null and void. The children thus became illegitimate and were automatically barred from all public office or honourable careers."[1]

Thus a decree, intended to eliminate a social evil, was now used to eliminate Protestants.

When the Spanish left and the Calvinists were in the majority the Civil Law in Belgium and Holland required that a mixed marriage be performed before the Calvinist minister only. In 1741 Pope Benedict XIV recognised mixed marriages without Roman Catholic priests being present[2]. This was extended to Ireland by Pius VI in 1785 and used in Ireland up to 1850.

In the 1680s, when Louis XIV was persecuting the Huguenots as a preliminary to revoking the Edict of Nantes Daniel Rops reports that:

"Mixed marriages were prohibited and children born of them were declared illegitimate and snatched from their parents to be brought up in the Catholic religion."[3]

Meanwhile, we have the Penal Laws in Ireland. These were modelled on the French anti-Huguenot laws. Up to 1793 it was a capital offence for a Roman Catholic priest to officiate at a mixed marriage. The last hanging was in 1726. From 1793 to 1833 this was reduced to a fine of £5,000. At the time the Roman Catholic Bishop of Ossory, later Archbishop of Dublin, John Troy said: "marriage between Protestants and Catholics is unlawful, wicked, and dangerous. The Penal Laws should not be repealed because they act as a deterrent."[4]

Medieval wedding

Thus, we see mixed marriages are **equally popular on both sides**.

The *Tametsi* decree was published in parts of Tuam Archdiocese in 1658, in other parts in 1745, but Galway city was an exception. It was ruled by a Warden in almost total independence of the Archbishop. Mixed marriages were considered in the city to be valid whether preformed in the Protestant or Catholic Church. Furthermore, no promise about the children was required. This somewhat confused situation led throughout Ireland to what historians call the *Galway Convention*, where the boys followed the father's and the girls the mother's denomination.[5] This ensured that land and property did not change denomination.

In 1850, the Synod of Thurles imposed on Ireland the equivalent of the future *Ne Temere* decree. A mixed marriage (a) needed a Papal Dispensation and (b) required that all the children be brought up as Roman Catholics. Both partners were required to make the promise verbally and in writing before witnesses. However, the regulations of Thurles were widely ignored. Furthermore, in 1852 the English Roman Catholic Bishops took the view that the dispensation should be from a parish priest and not Rome. When this was confirmed by Rome in 1853 the practice was widely taken up in Ireland. In 1858 Rome decreed that mixed marriages could not take place in church.

However, at the end of the nineteenth century the Vatican was on a 'tidy up' of all its legislation and one result was the *Ne Temere* (not casually) decree of 19th April 1908.

The result of this legislation was that both partners (a) promised to bring up all the children as Roman Catholic, (b) the Catholic partner worked to convert the other, and (c) the marriage could not take place in Church and there would be no ceremony, only the exchange of vows. Hungary and Germany were exempt until 1917. The decree was then universally applied on publication of the new Code of Canon Law [1917].

Ne Temere was enthusiastically applied by the Irish clergy. At the same time, we have civil unrest, a new border and civil war in Ireland. Dr Garrett Fitzgerald has shown, wearing his statistician's hat, that *Ne Temere* was the prime factor in reducing the Protestant population of the Irish Republic by 80%. At independence there was an initial exodus followed by the second phase of attrition using *Ne Temere*. Contrary to Roman Canon Law this was often applied retrospectively and marriages of long-standing were broken up. We can compare, in the same period, the 60% increase in the Roman Catholic population of Northern Ireland. Dr Fitzgerald asked the Irish Bishops to request Rome for a relaxation of *Ne Temere*, but they refused. Professor Oliver Rafferty SJ, Maynooth, has said that one of the Roman Catholic Church's most remarkable self-inflicted wounds was *Ne Temere*. It gave further evidence that Home Rule was indeed Rome Rule[6].

This is perhaps best understood by looking at the McCann case. Agnes and Alexander McCann were married in Antrim Presbyterian Church in May 1908. They moved to Belfast where Agnes worshipped at Townsend Street Presbyterian Church. By summer 1910, they had two children, Joseph and Mary. Alexander was informed by a parish priest that he was 'living in sin' and must marry in front of a priest. Agnes considered that they were properly married already and would not agree to this. In October 1910, Alexander and the two children disappeared. A distracted Mrs McCann roamed the streets of Belfast asking all she met if they had seen her babies. The case was widely publicised by her minister the Rev William Corkey. This was the first major outing of *Ne Temere* in Ulster and there were riots in the streets of Belfast, major public protest meetings in Belfast, Edinburgh, Glasgow, London, Dublin and Australia, Canada and New Zealand. Questions were asked in the House of Commons and a debate was held in the House of Lords. We now know that Alexander and the two children were assisted to move to the USA and settled near Pittsburgh. Agnes never again saw or heard from her husband or children.

Prior to 1910 the Presbyterian General Assembly had 30% of its members in favour of Home Rule, after the McCann case just 4%! The future Church of Ireland Archbishop of Dublin and Armagh John Gregg was then Dean in Cork. He said:

"The Protestant is to surrender every right of conscience that he possesses, except that he is graciously allowed to remain a Protestant himself, though he must submit to reasonable efforts to make a Romanist of him."

"If you hope to arrive at any reconciliation with Protestants, if you want to make even the thought of Home Rule not a nightmare to us, you will revolt against this portion of the decree: you will protest against it, you will drum it out of Cork, out of Ireland."

"It did look as if the barriers were becoming less unpassable; this uncalled-for decree from Italy has thrown national concord back by a hundred years."

"How can you expect us to trust ourselves to you? The decree is an attack on Irish Unity and can only make Protestants more irreconcilable to the idea of Home Rule."[8]

The hostility of the Orange Order to mixed marriage is overt and widely recognised. In 1916, the Grand Master of the Order, Colonel Wallace, declared that "the decree is final proof that Home Rule is Rome Rule."

A member entering a mixed marriage must leave the Order if any of the children are brought up as Roman Catholics, despite the claim that the Order stands for religious and civil liberty. This attitude is, of course, simply the mirror image of *Ne Temere.*

To quote Archbishop Donald Coggan of Canterbury (1967) referring to mixed marriage, "there can be few points of contact which are fraught with more potential opportunity – either for ecumenical advance or for discord". **In Ireland we usually opt for the discord**.

Even in 1941 Bishop Mageean of Down and Connor, at a Confirmation service in St Teresa's parish on Belfast's Glen Road,

Rev. D. Mageean

declared mixed marriage evil and boasted that in a neighbouring diocese no mixed marriage had taken place under four successive Bishops.[9]

In 1957 an Interchurch couple, Sheila and Sean Cloney, living in Fethard-on-Sea in south Wexford were visited by the local Roman Catholic clergy and informed that the children "will go to the Catholic school". The Church of Ireland wife disagreed with such an edict and took herself and the children to Belfast and on to Scotland. The local Catholics were convinced that a mere woman could not have managed this without help from her Protestant neighbours and relatives. They then instigated a boycott of the Protestant owned shops and farms. Even the elderly lady giving piano lessons had her young Catholic pupils withdrawn.

The main boycott lasted for five months, from the end of April 1957, although many local Catholics continued the boycott for many years. The local Roman Catholic Bishop completely supported the boycott and Bishop Browne of Galway preached on the virtues of the boycott. The local Knights of Saint Columbanus and the Gaelic Athletic Association policed and enforced the main boycott. De Valera eventually intervened to condemn the action, but again this outworking of the Irish Roman Catholic clergy's take on *Ne Temere* was being used to reinforce the message that Home Rule was indeed Rome Rule. Some readers may have seen the movie 'A Love Divided' made of this event.[10]

On a lighter note, Justin Keating, a future Dublin Labour Party Minister for Industry and Commerce, as a protest would go with a friend to Fethard to shop in Protestant shops and then to local pubs to purchase Jameson whiskey or Guinness. They would then say to the locals "you would boycott an elderly Protestant piano teacher, but you are drinking the Protestant drink." A swift exit usually followed!

Finally, in this sorry tale, we have the Tilson case in Dublin 1950. They were a mixed marriage couple recently working in Dublin. She ran off with another man leaving him with the three children. With no child minder available he put the children into a Protestant Children's Home until such times as he had child-care in place. She demanded the children be brought up as good Catholics like herself and went to the High Court. The judge ruled that the pre-nuptial agreement overruled the common law principle that the husband was the head of the family with the right to decide the religious upbringing. Judge Gavin Duffy ruled that the Irish Constitution articles 41, 42, and 44 gave precedent to Roman Canon Law over civil law. Of course, it was appealed to the Supreme Court where 4 of the 5 judges agreed with Judge Duffy's conclusion. The fifth, Judge Black, was the only Protestant judge on the Supreme Court.[11]

Things eased a little in 1966 when Rome issued *Matrimonii Sacramentum* which removed the requirement that the Catholic partner must "work prudently for the conversion of the non-Catholic spouse."

Pius X

I have not discussed the behaviour of the Protestant Churches in Ireland. This is because, with one exception, they have not been proactive, but rather reactive. The one occasion is the Anglican Roman Catholic International Commission [ARCIC] report on Marriage (1967) that was co-chaired by Archbishop George Simms of Armagh[12]. Their early reports were partially incorporated into new legislation arising from the Second Vatican Council, *Matrimonia Mixta* (1970). This now permitted the marriage in Church and required that only the RC partner need promise to do all, within his or her power **within the marriage**, to bring the children up as Roman Catholic.

Next in our historical survey is 1974 and the formation of the Northern Ireland Mixed Marriage Association [NIMMA]. This was the result of a weekend conference organised by Corrymeela for those interested, involved, or hoping to be involved in mixed marriage. The association developed four main aims:

1. Self help – pastoral care. With a few honourable exceptions among the clergy this did not exist elsewhere;

2. Provision of advice and information to other couples;

3. Help for clergy to fully understand mixed marriage;

4. Influence the local community's attitudes.

From 1995 to 2004 we were part-funded by the NI Community Relations Council with an office in Bryson House, Belfast. However, CRC then decided that we were no longer needed and funding ended. We have been funded since 2005 by the Dublin Department of Foreign Affairs Anglo-Irish Division's Reconciliation Fund.

There are many **sister organisations** around the world: England and Wales; Ireland; France; Germany; Italy; Austria; Switzerland; New Zealand; Australia; USA; Canada. All but France and Switzerland call themselves Associations of Interchurch Families. The modern **definitions** commonly used for mixed marriages include: both, one or neither partner practising. When both are practising, they are referred to as an Interchurch couple. NIMMA deliberately kept the options open for all to join. So by our definition, two humanists from perceived Protestant/Roman Catholic backgrounds are in a mixed marriage.

One unexpected outcome has been the **international dimension**. An international conference has been held every two years since 1980; hosted by NIMMA in 1982 and 1990. This has led to NIMMA having influence in Rome. The international committee has met the Pontifical Council in Rome to discuss the way forward and further meetings are planned. The Council has asked that, initially, local Bishops' Conferences should be approached to obtain practical changes in their areas. NIMMA continues to argue for changes in the approach to baptism, Eucharistic sharing and education.

The Position Today:

I want to look at the influence mixed marriage couples have had on the Churches and will first quote Bishop Samuel Poyntz, at that time C of I Bishop of Cork, at an Interchurch meeting in Ballymascanlon in 1984:

"It must be encouragement to many involved in the sometimes lonely tension of a two-church marriage to realise that over the years the Churches have not managed to change the couple, rather have the couple done much to change the characteristic attitudes of the Churches."

This is most clearly seen in the Roman Catholic Directory on Mixed Marriages in Ireland (1983)[13]. NIMMA made written and oral submissions and six of our eight proposals were accepted.

The agreed proposals were:

1: Joint Pastoral Care from both clergy acting together.

2: The appointment of Diocesan specialists. This has been a great success.

3: The wedding should take place in the bride's Church – the social norm.

4: There would not normally be a nuptial mass. To declare the couple united in marriage and then disunited at the Eucharist is theological nonsense.

5: Both clergy to be present at the wedding, robed and taking an active part.

6: A proper understanding of the Promise.

The two proposals refused were Eucharistic sharing and concelebrated baptism. I will expand on only one, the Promise. This is the most contentious and the one that has caused the most damage to community relations in the past 100 years.

The original promise read:

"I declare that I am resolved, as God's law demands, to preserve my Catholic faith, and to avoid all danger of falling away from it. Moreover, I sincerely undertake and I will, as God's law requires, do everything possible, as far as in me lies, to have all of the children of our marriage baptised and brought up in the Catholic faith."

This has undergone some change and the Catholic partner is now asked:

"Do you promise to do what you can within the unity of your marriage to have all of the children of your marriage baptised and brought up in the Catholic faith?"

This is more understandable and much more user friendly, but what does it mean?

The Directory itsself states in section 8.1 that: "The religious upbringing of the children is the joint responsibility of both parents. The obligations of the Catholic party do not, and cannot, cancel out or in any way call into question, the conscientious duties of the other party."

Section 8.5 continues " Nonetheless, the decision about the education of the children does not belong to the Catholic party alone. The actual circumstances of the marriage form the context in which this obligation must be carried out and these circumstances are bound to vary considerably. The possibility exists that the Catholic will be in a situation where some or all of the children are brought up in the denomination of the other party."

Thus **now** the upbringing of the children is the **sole responsibility of the parents** to do what is right for them in their marriage. A major grievance has now been removed.

We also need to look at the wider international scene. While the general theological aspects are similar the world over, the living conditions do differ considerably. In Northern Ireland, we have 90% segregated housing, 94% segregated schools, separate teacher training colleges, separate games and separate dances/pubs. These conditions do not exist anywhere else in the world, though they once did in the White-controlled South Africa and, of course, in some southern states of the United States. This has resulted in NIMMA being involved, in association with Housing Trusts and the NI Housing Executive, to provide reserved housing in neutral areas for mixed marriage couples - an alien concept to the rest of the world. NIMMA's continual lobbying and our representation on the NIHE Housing Advisory Committee has helped bring about the 'Shared Neighbourhood Programme', which has developed 30 shared neighbourhoods across the Province over a three year period.

[Shared neighbourhoods are where people choose to live with others, regardless of religion or race, in an area that is safe and welcoming to all. NIMMA's determination to pursue, for 20 years, shared social housing grew out of our experiences in providing advice and practical help to couples facing intimidation.]

To obtain housing or employment the applicant is generally required to state their perceived religion, but the children of Interchurch couples would argue that they are not **either** but **both**. Housing associations and the Civil Service have not found this a comfortable concept. Indeed, refusal to tick one box or to tick both boxes means that a Civil Service job application will be refused. Is this the way to a shared future? As this was being written, the NIHE application form was changed to include a tick box for dual church membership!

Many people would consider that with the present state of religious practice, mixed marriages are no longer a problem. Unfortunately, this is not the case. We still have our dinosaur clergy and laity.

For example in the recent past we have had the problem of:

(1) a couple visiting the parish priest to discuss their wedding plans. When he discovered that the non-Roman Catholic would not be converting on marriage, he declared the couple 'evil' and asked them to leave;

(2) a Church of Ireland rector refused to discuss a mixed marriage with one of his parishioners;

(3) community relations are not good west of the Bann, but sympathetic Roman Catholic clergy working there have asked us to help the Presbyterian clergy deal positively with mixed marriage couples.

Laity continue to be a problem, with many demanding that the grandchildren be baptised into their denomination, irrespective of the wishes of the couple. In Ireland, both north and south, land and property have often acquired denominational labels and couples are told that they will not inherit the farm or business if the marriage goes ahead.

Lest anyone think that I have been pessimistic, this is not the case. We have made much progress over the past 38 years as a reading of the stories in this book will demonstrate. The number of mixed relationships in Northern Ireland is increasing steadily, with more mixing thanks to fair employment legislation, Integrated Schools and a desire by most of the wider community for a shared future.

Before the Belfast Agreement, the number of couples calling NIMMA went up because most politicians do not lead, but follow the electorate. Thus, the rate of new mixed relationships is a good measure of the success of reconciliation in the community.

Indeed we cannot and will not have true peace until all can feel free to inter-marry if they so wish.

Further details on mixed relationships and the work of NIMMA can be obtained from our web site WWW.NIMMA.ORG.UK
or by email to nimma@nireland.com
or by phone to our office 028 9023 5444

References

1. *History of the Belgians*, A de Meeus, Praeger New York 1962.

2. Mixed marriage and Irish politics: the effect of *Ne Temere*, Eoin de Bhaldraithe, *Studies*, Autumn 1988.

3. *The Church in the Seventeenth Century*, Daniel-Rops, London: Dent 1963.

4. *Priests and People in Pre-Famine Ireland, 1780-1845*, SJ Connolly. Gill and Macmillan, 2001.

5. *The Wardens of Galway*, RJ Kelly, J of the Roy Soc Antiquarians, Ireland 1896.

6. *Catholicism in Ulster* 1603-1983, Oliver P Rafferty SJ. Gill and Macmillan, 1994.

7. *Glad did I live*, William Corkey, The Belfast News-Letter Ltd, Belfast, 1962

8. *The Ne Temere Decree*, JF Gregg. APCK, Dublin, 1911

9. *On this day*, E Phoenix. The Irish News, June 17, 2010

10. *The Fethard-on-Sea Boycott*, T Fanning. The Collins Press, 2010.

11. *Church and State in Modern Ireland*, JH Whyte. Gill and Macmillan, 1980.

12. *George Otto Simms*, L Whiteside. Colin Smythe Ltd, 1990.

13. *Directory on Mixed Marriage*, Irish Episcopal Conference. Veritas Dub. 1983.

Further Reading

Beyond Tolerance: The Challenge of Mixed Marriage, Ed Fr M Hurley, Chapman London, 1975.

Two Churches One Love, Rev A Heron. APCK 1977.

Mixed Marriage in Ireland, A companion for those involved or about to be involved in a mixed marriage, NIMMA, 3rd edition 2003.

Interchurch Marriage in Ireland, A &W Odling-Smee. Catalyst, 2001.

For the impact of *Ne Temere* on Ireland *see*
Fr Ralph, G O'Donovan. Macmillan and Co London, 1913
Waiting, G O'Donovan. Macmillan and Co London, 1914